FEB 1 5 2004

Withdrawn

TRAILBLAZERS of the MODERN WORLD

MARTIN LUTHER KING JR.

By Adele Q. Brown

BLOOMINGDALE PUBLIC LIBRARY
101 FAIRFIELD WAY
BLOOMINGDALE, IL 60108
630 - 529 - 3120

WORLD ALMANAC® LIBRARY

Please visit our web site at: **www.worldalmanaclibrary.com**
For a free color catalog describing World Almanac® Library's list
of high-quality books and multimedia programs, call 1-800-848-2928 (USA)
or 1-800-387-3178 (Canada). World Almanac® Library's fax: (414) 332-3567.

Library of Congress Cataloging-in-Publication Data

Brown, Adele Q.
    Martin Luther King Jr. / by Adele Q. Brown.
       p. cm. — (Trailblazers of the modern world)
    Includes bibliographical references and index.
    Summary: Describes the life and career of Dr. Martin Luther King, Jr., including his accomplishments
in the civil rights movement and his impact on American history.
    ISBN 0-8368-5091-2 (lib. bdg.)
    ISBN 0-8368-5251-6 (softcover)
    1. King, Martin Luther, Jr., 1929-1968—Juvenile literature. 2. African Americans—Biography—Juvenile
literature. 3. Civil rights workers—United States—Biography—Juvenile literature. 4. Baptists—United
States—Clergy—Biography—Juvenile literature. 5. African Americans—Civil rights—History—20th century—
Juvenile literature. [1. King, Martin Luther, Jr., 1929-1968. 2. Civil rights workers. 3. Clergy. 4. Civil rights
movements—History. 5. African Americans—Biography.] I. Title. II. Series.
E185.97.K5B74   2003
323'.092—dc21
[B]   2003042295

First published in 2004 by
World Almanac® Library
330 West Olive Street, Suite 100
Milwaukee, WI 53212 USA

Copyright © 2004 by World Almanac® Library.

Project manager: Jonny Brown
Editor: Betsy Rasmussen
Design and page production: Scott M. Krall
Photo research: Diane Laska-Swanke
Indexer: Walter Kronenberg

Photo credits: © AP/Wide World Photos: 4, 6, 9 top, 18, 25 top, 32, 35, 38, 41, 43 bottom; © Bettmann/CORBIS: 10,
15, 20 top, 21, 26, 28, 29, 33, 37, 39, 40, 42; © Sean Gallup/Getty Images: 43 top; © Shel Hershorn UT Austin/Hulton
Archive/Getty Images: 25 bottom; © Hulton Archive/Getty Images: cover, 5 both, 7, 9 bottom, 13, 14, 16, 17, 20
bottom, 22, 23, 30, 31, 34; © Flip Schulke/CORBIS: 8

All rights reserved. No part of this book may be reproduced, stored in a retrieval system, or transmitted in any form
or by any means, electronic, mechanical, photocopying, recording, or otherwise, without the prior written permission
of the copyright holder.

Printed in the United States of America

1 2 3 4 5 6 7 8 9 07 06 05 04 03

TABLE of CONTENTS

Words that appear in the glossary are printed in **boldface**
type the first time they occur in the text.

CHAPTER 1

A GIFTED AND INSPIRING LEADER

Negro, Black, or African American

In the middle of the last century, most people (including Martin Luther King Jr.) referred to African Americans as *Negroes*. In this book, the word *Negro* is used when quoting Dr. King or others from that time period. In the rest of the text, two terms are used that are acceptable today—*black* and *African American*.

In 1963, one hundred years after President Abraham Lincoln granted freedom to all slaves, Americans celebrated that anniversary. That summer, Dr. Martin Luther King Jr. addressed the nation from the Lincoln Memorial in Washington, D.C. "One hundred years later the Negro is still not free," he declared. "One hundred years later the life of the Negro is still sadly crippled by the **manacles** of **segregation** and the chains of **discrimination**. . . . One hundred years later the Negro . . . finds himself an **exile** in his own land."

On March 22, 1956, Dr. King was fined $500 for organizing a peaceful protest against segregation. That night he told a crowd of supporters, "The protest is still on."

THE WAY THINGS WERE

Dr. King was right. Little had changed for African Americans, and they did not enjoy the same rights and privileges as whites. In southern states, the situation was especially bad. The lives of black people there were tightly controlled by **Jim Crow laws**, which denied equal rights to blacks and prevented them from mixing freely with whites. African Americans were kept separate on buses and trains and in schools, stores, hospitals, parks, restaurants, and many other places. "Colored only" signs were posted in places where blacks were allowed entrance.

Many white southerners felt comfortable with segregation. They wanted to keep African Americans at a distance and in **inferior** positions. Black citizens, on the other hand, felt humiliated and degraded by the way they were treated. Of his own experiences with segregation, Dr. King once said, "I could never adjust to the separate waiting rooms, separate eating places, separate rest rooms, partly because the separate was always unequal, and partly because the very idea of separation did something to my sense of dignity and self-respect."

From his early twenties on, Dr. King was determined to help black people regain dignity and self-respect. A stirring speaker and man of tremendous courage, vision, and intelligence, he soon became a great leader. His words and deeds inspired millions of African Americans to believe in themselves and their right to equal treatment under the law. Armed with those beliefs, African Americans began to oppose the racial discrimination that had caused them so much pain for so long.

King, his colleagues, and their followers worked hard to abolish Jim Crow laws, but the job was difficult. In the 1950s, blacks did not dare disagree with whites for fear of punishment. With Dr. King's inspirational words and heroic work as an example, however, they began to challenge segregation laws courageously.

When this picture was taken in 1961, African Americans who lived in the Deep South were not allowed to use the same public waiting rooms as whites.

In 1965, Martin Luther King Jr. led a 54-mile- (87-kilometer-) long march to publicize discrimination against black Americans.

NONVIOLENCE MAKES A DIFFERENCE

One of the greatest ideas Dr. King brought to the **civil rights** movement was that of nonviolent resistance. He and his followers peacefully protested the unfairness of segregation, while tolerating abusive name-calling, arrest, jail, and even beatings. Dr. King's group did not physically

fight back. "We will march nonviolently," King told his supporters. "We will force this nation, this city, this world, to face its own conscience. . . . The struggle is not between black and white. But between good and evil."

Dr. King led his nonviolent civil rights campaign by marching, writing, and giving speeches. With his mastery of words and a strong belief in the power of love, he won many admirers. "Love builds up and unites," he said. "Hate tears down and destroys. . . . Yes, love—which means understanding. . . [and] goodwill, even for one's enemies—is the solution to the race problem."

KING'S LASTING LEGACY

King's practice of nonviolence achieved lasting results. Two laws that secured the rights of African Americans—the Civil Rights Act of 1964 and the Voting Rights Act of 1965—were enacted largely because of demonstrations and protests by Dr. King and his followers. And in the decades since his death, the goals he worked for have not been forgotten. His organization, associates, and family still strive to bring about social change through nonviolent means.

Today, we are often reminded of the changes King set in motion. While the problem of racial discrimination still exists, laws now uphold equal rights for persons of all colors, races, genders, and religions. As a result, African Americans are free to socialize with whom they please, shop and attend schools where they like, and pursue personal dreams. Dr. King's vision helped both black and white Americans realize that their futures must be united, not separate.

A sculpture in Indianapolis, Indiana, honors Dr. King and Robert F. Kennedy, a U.S. Attorney General who actively supported King's work.

artin Luther King Jr. was the great-grandson of a slave. That slave, Jim Long, was freed after the Civil War (1861–1865), and he and his family then worked as **sharecroppers** on farms owned by white people. Sharecroppers worked hard but rarely made enough money to pay their bills. Farmers often took advantage of a sharecropper's lack of education and treated him or her badly. Unfortunately, Jim's family had no other skills. It was not until the early 1900s that one of Jim Long's grandsons, Michael (Mike) Luther King, found a better way to earn a living.

For these African Americans living in the Deep South, life was little better in 1900 than it had been during slavery.

Taking Advantage

After watching a white farmer cheat his father, Mike King reminded his dad to ask about money owed him for cotton seed—the most valuable income for a sharecropper. When his father asked, the farmer grudgingly paid King, but the farmer was furious because Mike had caught him trying to steal from his father. After that, the farmer kicked the Kings off his land. Without a job, Mike's father turned to drinking and abused his wife and son. His father's behavior caused Mike to leave home at age fourteen.

Mike ran away from home when he was fourteen and took odd jobs to support himself. In 1918, at age nineteen, he became a minister. He moved to Atlanta,

Georgia, and founded a church. Wanting to improve his education, Mike returned to school. He entered fifth grade at age twenty-one, and he eventually graduated from both high school and college.

In 1926, Mike married Alberta Williams. Their daughter Chris was born first, and then on January 15, 1929, Michael Luther King Jr. was born. They called their son M.L. for short. His full name was later changed to Martin Luther King Jr. Another boy, Alfred Daniel (A.D.), was born into the family three years later.

Michael to Martin

Until he was four years old, Martin Luther King Jr.'s first name was Michael, the same as his father's. In 1933, the boy's father decided to change their first names to Martin. After that, father and son were both known as Martin Luther King, although they kept their nicknames, M.L. and Mike.

When M.L. was two years old, his father became pastor of the Ebenezer Baptist Church. By then, Reverend King was influential in Atlanta's African

Ebenezer Baptist Church in Atlanta, Georgia.

American community, and he and his family lived in the prosperous all-black neighborhood of Sweet Auburn.

RACIAL BAPTISM

Due to Jim Crow laws, M.L. did not have a chance to get to know many white people. In fact, he had only one white friend—the son of a nearby grocer. In 1935, his friendship

The house in which Martin Luther King Jr. was born.

"I Am a Man"

M.L.'s father taught him not to be afraid to maintain his dignity and stand up for his rights. One day, a white policeman spoke disrespectfully to Reverend King, saying, "Listen, boy. . ." The reverend interrupted the officer right away. He pointed to his son and said, "That is a boy. I am a man, and until you call me one, I will not listen to you."

M.L. often heard his father telling white store owners that he would not go to the back of the store, where African Americans were expected to shop out of view of white shoppers. "We'll either buy shoes sitting here or we won't buy shoes at all," King Sr. once told a shopkeeper.

In the mid-1930s, many of Atlanta's African Americans did not live as comfortably as the King family.

with that boy ended. It happened one afternoon, when M.L. went to his friend's house to play. When he arrived, the grocer announced that his son could no longer play with him. M.L. was surprised and hurt. He did not yet understand that the color of his skin had affected his

friendship. Later that day, Mrs. King reassured her son. "You are as good as anyone else," she told him. "Don't ever forget that." Then M.L.'s mother told him about the terrible wrongs of slavery, racial prejudice, and segregation.

Much later, King recalled, "My parents would always tell me that I should not hate the white man . . . that it was my duty as a Christian to love him. [But] how could I love a race of people . . . who had been responsible for breaking me up with one of my best childhood friends? This was a great question in my mind for a number of years."

Dr. Martin Luther King Sr. preaching.

BAPTIST LIFE

M.L. was a smart and competitive child. In fact, he insisted on being **baptized** when he was only five years old because he had just seen his older sister, Chris, join the faith. He later admitted, "I would not let her get ahead of me so I was next."

Religion was an important part of the family's life. M.L. loved to hear Bible stories, and he sang gospel songs in front of audiences. All three of the King children learned to recite scripture and sing hymns. As they grew older, they took piano lessons and joined the choir at Ebenezer Baptist Church.

M.L.'s parents were loving but strict. King later recalled, "I grew up in a family where love was central and where lovely relationships were ever present." Each child had duties and responsibilities, and failure to take care of them brought punishment. Reverend King did not tolerate disobedient or disrespectful behavior from anyone, including his children.

AN EARLY EDUCATION

Mother Dear, as Mrs. King was called, was a teacher, so she taught her young children to read at home. M.L. learned quickly and loved words. Reverend King recalled that after attending a sermon given by a minister known for his eloquence, M.L. said, "Daddy, that man had some big words. When I grow up I'm going to get me some big words."

By 1934, M.L. read so well that Mrs. King enrolled him in first grade a year early. The school soon discovered that he was too young and made him wait another year. Back at home, he continued to read books from his father's library and the public library. When he was older, he started a paper route to earn money to buy his own books.

In school, M.L. was quiet, sensitive, and studious. He was a good reader and a good writer but a terrible speller. He liked to dress well and soon earned the nickname "Tweedie," after the tweed sports jackets he wore. He also enjoyed opera music, joined the debating team, and liked girls and dancing. His father, however, did not approve of the girls or the dancing.

King was such a good student that he skipped ninth and twelfth grades. When he was only fifteen, he graduated from high school. His father hoped he would join the ministry after that, but M.L. wanted to go to college.

A Winner Loses His Seat

In 1944, when King was a junior at Booker T. Washington High School, he represented his school in a speaking competition. He and a teacher traveled more than two hours by bus to attend the debate. His speech, "The Negro and the Constitution," won first prize.

Later, as they rode home on the bus, the driver told M.L. to give his seat to a white person. This order made the boy angry, and he refused to get up. Wanting to avoid trouble, M.L.'s teacher asked him to come to the rear of the bus, where black people were expected to sit. King got up but then saw that there were no empty seats. He later recalled, "We stood up in the aisle for ninety miles to Atlanta. That night will never leave my memory. It was the angriest I have ever been in my life."

CHAPTER 3

YOUNG MAN WITH A FUTURE

When M.L graduated from high school in 1944, World War II (1939–1945) was raging. Many black teenagers had already enlisted in the military, but King wanted to continue his education. In the fall, he enrolled in Atlanta's Morehouse College, the all-black institution his father had attended.

A Segregated Military

Until 1948, black soldiers served in segregated units of the U.S. military. Those units performed many acts of heroism in World War II, including bombing raids by the all-black Tuskegee Airmen and the defense of France by the all-black 614th Tank Destroyer Battalion. Even though black soldiers performed the same duties as whites, racial discrimination was pervasive. In fact, the U.S. military put white southern officers in charge of black units and supported the idea that black soldiers were inferior

Jackie Robinson, the first African American to play in major league baseball, served as an officer in the segregated U.S. Army. He once said, "I felt there were two wars raging at once—one against foreign enemies and one against domestic foes [those who thought blacks were inferior]—and the black man was forced to fight both."

The Tuskeegee Airmen were black, but their leader was white.

As a fifteen-year-old college freshman, Martin Luther King Jr. was three years younger than his classmates. Despite the age difference, he worked hard to fit in. He even played football—a challenging sport for a boy who wasn't very large physically. King was never a top student at Morehouse, but he impressed his teachers with his speaking ability and his quick mind.

SUMMER JOBS AND NORTHERN LIFE

During summer breaks, King worked to help pay for his college education. In 1944, his first summer job took him to Connecticut, where he labored outside in the tobacco fields. He had never been to northern states before, and he was both curious and nervous. The first thing he learned in Connecticut was that blacks were treated differently in the North. There were no "colored only" or "white only" signs there. He could go into public parks, eat at lunch counters, and shop at stores with white customers. He later recalled, "I had never thought that a person of my race could eat anywhere, but we ate in one of the finest restaurants in Hartford."

When that summer ended and he returned home, M.L. had trouble readjusting. "It was a bitter feeling going back to segregation," he wrote. "It was hard to understand why I could ride wherever I pleased on the train from New York to Washington [D.C.] and then had to change to a Jim Crow car at the nation's capital in order to continue the trip to Atlanta. The first time that I was seated behind a curtain in a dining car, I felt as if the curtain had been dropped on my selfhood."

Picking tobacco in Connecticut.

Over the next few summers, King worked as a laborer loading trucks in Atlanta. The work did not always go smoothly for him, and he quit his first job when a white boss called him a "nigger." At work, he experienced the financial reality that faced all black workers—the fact that they were paid less than whites for doing the same work. King's experiences in those jobs strengthened his belief that racism and Jim Crow laws were unjust and evil. They also helped him see that racism was part of a larger economic system.

DISCOVERING NEW IDEAS

Martin Luther King Jr. began to think about how he might help change the way African Americans were treated by whites. After talking with Morehouse president Dr. Benjamin Mays, King realized that his religious and social ideas were compatible. At the invitation of his father, M.L. delivered his first sermon at Ebenezer Baptist Church in 1946. The sermon was a big success, and King had found his path.

Rev. Dr. Benjamin Elijah Mays.

In 1948, at age nineteen, M.L. was ordained as a Baptist minister and became known as Reverend Martin Luther King Jr. That same year, he graduated from Morehouse College. Instead of immediately joining his father at Ebenezer Baptist Church, however, King entered Crozer Theological Seminary in Pennsylvania to pursue his religious studies.

Crozer had a small campus and King was one of only six black students. The color of his skin did not matter to his classmates, and he enjoyed campus life. While at Crozer, King dropped his childhood nickname M.L., preferring to be called Martin instead.

King threw himself into his studies and did well. By the time he graduated in 1951, he was the president of his senior class. He received the prize as Crozer's outstanding student and a fellowship of thirteen hundred dollars to continue his studies. As before, his father hoped that Martin would join him at Ebenezer Baptist Church, but Martin went north to Boston instead.

Filled with commitment and a sense of purpose, King began to explore the ideas of many **philosophers**.

Mahatma Gandhi during a protest march in India in 1930.

The Great Gandhi

Mohandas "Mahatma" Gandhi (1869–1948) was a deeply spiritual man who led India to freedom from British rule in 1948. He and his followers achieved independence for India without force, using only nonviolent resistance—**boycotts** of English products, protest marches, and other peaceful methods. Almost entirely without bloodshed, Gandhi's quiet revolution put an end to British colonial occupation.

Martin Luther King Jr. was transformed by Gandhi's ideas about nonviolent confrontation. He was especially impressed by Gandhi's power to lead people with words instead of weapons.

Mohandas Gandhi and Henry David Thoreau were two men whose writings introduced King to the idea of nonviolent opposition to social wrongs. It was an idea that appealed to him greatly. The more he read, the more he began to think that nonviolent methods might work for African Americans in their struggle for equality and respect.

Henry David Thoreau.

An Original Thinker

At Crozer, King studied the writings of the nineteenth-century American philosopher Henry David Thoreau (1817–1862). In his 1849 essay, "Civil Disobedience," Thoreau explained that citizens have a right to disobey certain laws that are unjust or evil. King also discovered that Thoreau had opposed slavery long before the Civil War and had gone to jail rather than obey a law he believed was unfair. Many years later, Gandhi and then King would make the same personal sacrifice.

CHAPTER 4

FORMING A VISION

In 1951, Martin Luther King Jr. began pursuing a graduate degree in philosophy at Boston University. While studying there, he continued to sharpen his speaking skills and religious ideas by delivering guest sermons at churches around the city. "Even when he was so young," his future wife observed, "he drew people to him from the very first moment with his eloquence, his sincerity, and his moral stature."

MARRIAGE AND FAMILY

It was in Boston that King fell in love with Coretta Scott. The two were married on June 18, 1953, in her hometown of Marion, Alabama. Since neither had completed their studies, the newlyweds returned to Boston. Coretta received her music degree there in 1954, and

Coretta Scott King and Dr. Martin Luther King Jr. in 1956.

her husband received his doctorate degree a short time later, adding the title of Doctor to his name.

In the fall of 1954, Dr. King accepted the pastorship of Dexter Avenue Baptist Church in Montgomery, Alabama. He was twenty-five years old and was already the highest paid clergyman in Montgomery's black community.

About one year after moving to Montgomery, the Kings' first child, Yolanda, was born. Just two weeks later, however, a racist incident shifted King's attention away from his family and to his calling. It all started on a city bus.

In the early 1950s, many African Americans in Montgomery used the bus to get to and from work or school. Unfortunately, they often were treated badly by white bus drivers. This left the black community feeling humiliated and angry, but they were unsure as to how to make changes. There seemed to be only two choices— either they could find other transportation, or they could challenge the Jim Crow laws. Unfortunately, neither choice seemed practical. First, most black bus riders could not afford any other kind of transportation. Second, disobeying the law could surely anger some whites (it had in the past), and that could result in physical attacks on blacks.

"Brown v. Board of Education"

In October 1954, shortly before the Kings moved to Montgomery, Alabama, the U.S. Supreme Court "unanimously outlawed racial segregation in the nation's public schools" in its Brown v. Board of Education decision. This historic ruling ended the practice of sending black and white children to separate schools. From that moment forward, black and white students were to learn together, side by side, in the same classrooms.

Back of the Bus

By the 1950s, African Americans in the South had been badly treated on buses. They were expected to pay at the front of the bus, turn around and get off the bus, and then re-enter through the back staircase. Humiliating as that was, they did it. Even worse, bus drivers sometimes sped off, leaving behind black riders who had just paid and were walking to the rear of the bus to reboard.

Also, on Montgomery buses, African Americans in the first ten rows had to give up their seats to whites if another seat was free for the black rider. Drivers, however, paid no attention to the details of this rule. They often ordered blacks to give their seats to whites no matter where they were sitting or whether or not another seat was available.

Rosa Parks sitting in the front of a bus in December 1956.

On December 1, 1955, a seemingly small incident triggered a major protest. That day, an African-American woman named Rosa Parks got on a Montgomery bus and sat in the eleventh row. When a white man boarded, the driver ordered her and three other blacks to move to the back of the bus. Mrs. Parks refused. The driver became angry and called the police. When they arrived, they arrested Rosa.

BOYCOTT

News of the arrest spread quickly in the black community. Local black leaders—Dr. Martin Luther King Jr., Reverend Ralph Abernathy of the First Baptist Church, and several others—met to discuss the situation. They decided to use Mrs. Parks's arrest to challenge the legal basis for segregating black passengers on buses.

While their lawyers took the issue to court, King, Abernathy, and the others talked about how they might put pressure on the bus company to change the way drivers treated black riders. They soon realized that if all paying black passengers refused to ride buses, the white owners of the bus line in Montgomery would lose money.

They also reasoned that if no black riders went downtown, white shop owners would have no black customers. Finally, they figured that when whites started losing money, they would understand that they needed to treat black customers more respectfully just to stay in business. With those thoughts in mind

Rev. Ralph Abernathy.

and with Mrs. Parks's arrest upsetting the community, the black leaders decided to organize a one-day boycott of the Montgomery bus system.

On Monday, December 5, 1955, the boycott went into effect. Amazingly, more than 85 percent of black riders did not use the buses. It was the first time the city's African-American community had been so unified. That same day, their leaders decided to form a civil rights group—the Montgomery Improvement Association (MIA). The new association elected Dr. Martin Luther King Jr. president and Reverend Ralph Abernathy program chairman.

On Monday night, nearly five thousand supporters cheered the two ministers. Describing the scene, Abernathy recalled, "I don't think I have ever heard a more joyous sound in my life, and as I looked over at Martin I knew he felt the same extraordinary sense of unity among our people. . . . We both knew that we were on the brink of a great victory."

Police officers arresting Dr. King in 1958.

A NONVIOLENT BEGINNING

That evening, King asked the crowd to continue the boycott to protest segregation on Montgomery's city buses. People overwhelmingly agreed. Then King preached about the importance of nonviolence. According to Abernathy, King asked them "to go into the streets and to accept whatever punishment the white community had to offer, whether jail or beating or death." Abernathy reflected, "We were asking them to take this risk without ever raising a hand in their own defense."

It turned out that King was one of the first targets of boycott-related violence. On January 30, 1956, some-

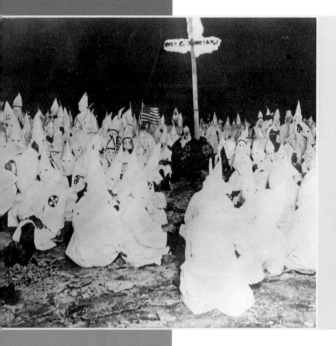

Living with Terror

Until the mid-twentieth century, if you were black and lived in the South, you were probably fearful of whites. You had good reason to be. White segregationists—some of whom were members of secret societies such as the **Ku Klux Klan**—terrorized black citizens. They burned crosses in front of the homes of African Americans, bombed black churches, and **lynched** black citizens. These violent crimes against African Americans rarely resulted in arrests.

Members of the Ku Klux Klan often wore white robes and hats. They also wore masks to conceal their identities.

one threw a bomb into King's home. Mrs. King and baby Yolanda were inside, but neither was hurt. When King arrived, he found an angry crowd of black supporters on his front lawn. To their surprise, King was neither bitter nor angry. "I want you to go home and put down your weapons," he told them. "We cannot solve this problem through retaliatory violence. We must meet violence with nonviolence. . . . We must meet hate with love." The crowd left, and the entire country marveled at Dr. King's powerful message of love in the face of such violent hatred. His words set the tone for the tough days ahead.

No one knew how long the boycott would last, so the black community got prepared. The MIA sponsored workshops about nonviolent protest and helped blacks travel around the city. African-American churches bought automobiles to use as taxis. Black people began carpooling, walking, hitchhiking, and riding bicycles.

Montgomery's African Americans avoided buses for more than a year. Then, in November 1956, they won an important victory. The U.S. Supreme Court ruled that segregation on Montgomery city buses was illegal. When news of the official ruling reached Montgomery on December 20, 1956, the ordeal was over. Their nonviolent protest had taken 382 days—longer than anyone had dreamed—but it had achieved open bus seating and job opportunities for black people at the bus company.

TERRORISM RESULTS IN UNITY

Unfortunately, the situation in Montgomery worsened after the Supreme Court outlawed segregation on buses. Just days later, the Ku Klux Klan went on a rampage, shooting one pregnant black woman, beating another, and burning crosses. Then, in January 1957, Reverend Abernathy's home was bombed. His First Baptist Church and two others were also bombed. Local police made little effort to find the criminals.

Those displays of violence saddened King. Speaking at a prayer meeting, he offered his own life to the civil rights cause. "Lord," he prayed, "I hope no one will have to die as a result of this struggle for freedom in Montgomery. Certainly, I don't want to die. But if anyone has to die, let it be me, Lord." That speech energized the community. People saw a martyr, heard a leader, and rallied once more behind the young, twenty-eight-year-old Baptist minister. They hoped he would lead them to freedom.

The events that occurred in Montgomery made national headlines. That exposure helped carry the civil rights message across the United States. The media often quoted King's nonviolent messages, and his beautiful, inspiring words increased support for the cause.

In 1957, Dr. King addressed a crowd of thousands from the steps of the Lincoln Memorial in Washington, D.C.

CHAPTER 5

A VOCAL REFORMER

By early 1957, Martin Luther King Jr. had been featured on the cover of national magazines. He had spoken many times on radio and television. And when King spoke, people listened.

THE SOUTHERN CHRISTIAN LEADERSHIP COUNCIL

While the press focused on King, southern civil rights groups stayed busy organizing their ranks. In 1957, several of those organizations, including the Montgomery Improvement Association, banded together to form the Southern Christian Leadership Council (SCLC). The new association elected Dr. King as their president.

The SCLC's first goal was to secure the right to vote for African Americans in southern states. Toward that end, the SCLC's lawyers started going to court to challenge unfair voting registration laws. Meanwhile, Dr. King and Abernathy led a voter registration campaign. Under their leadership, thousands of volunteers went to black neighborhoods to help people register. More than one million new African-American voters registered by 1958.

No Vote, No Power

Voting equals power. Wanting to keep African Americans from gaining power, white politicians in the South passed laws to keep them from registering to vote. According to those laws, citizens could register only if they could pass a written test or pay a tax. Since many southern blacks were uneducated and poor, they could not meet the registration requirements. Without the vote, they had no voice in the government and no way to change laws that discriminated against them.

Between 1958 and 1960, Dr. King kept a hectic schedule that included organizing, writing, speaking, traveling, and preaching. In 1959, however, it all became too much, and King resigned as pastor of Montgomery's Dexter Avenue Baptist Church. He then moved his family to Atlanta, Georgia, the home of the SCLC's main office.

When they moved to Georgia, Dr. and Mrs. King had two children, Yolanda (Yoki) and Martin III (Marty). Within the next few years, Dexter and Bernice were born. King juggled the needs of his family with his work at the SCLC and preaching at his father's church, Ebenezer Baptist.

Dr. King holding one of his books.

STUDENTS FOR FREEDOM

In 1960, black college students became active in the civil rights movement. Tired of not being served at "white only" food establishments, they conducted **sit-ins** throughout the South. Their determination and patience impressed King, who helped them form an offshoot of the SCLC called the Student Nonviolent Coordinating Committee (SNCC).

In May 1961, the SNCC tested the laws governing bus travel between states. Black and white students boarded two buses traveling south from Washington, D.C., to Montgomery, Alabama. They called the bus trips "Freedom Rides." The Freedom Rides

Whites often came to watch black sit-ins in the late 1950s.

Student Sit-ins

In February 1960, a few black college students from Greensboro, North Carolina, began a protest by sitting at a "white only" lunch counter and waiting to be served. They were polite and quiet, but no one served them. They returned day after day with the same outcome: no food and no service. News about their protest encouraged more sit-ins. Soon black and white students were holding sit-ins to protest segregated restaurants in many southern cities.

The sit-ins were nonviolent on the part of the protesters. Even when white hecklers dumped ketchup on their heads, threw food at them, and burned them with cigarettes, the students did not physically fight back. Eventually, store owners lost income because the bad publicity from the sit-ins drove away customers. The owners finally relented and agreed to serve blacks and whites together at lunch counters.

In 1961, the National Guard was sent to Montgomery, Alabama to keep peace between the races.

angered segregationists, and violent white mobs attacked both buses in Alabama. They set one bus on fire and assaulted the fleeing, unarmed students. Many freedom riders were hospitalized with serious injuries. King arrived and tried to lift their spirits: "We are going to be calm and we are going to stand up for what we know is right. Alabama will have to face the fact that we are determined to be free. . . . Fear not, we've come too far to turn back." King also urged U.S. Attorney General Robert Kennedy to protect the students. Kennedy responded by sending federal marshals to restore peace. His marshals accompanied the students as they continued their Freedom Rides.

"Segregation now! Segregation tomorrow! Segregation forever!" Those were the fighting words of Alabama Governor George C. Wallace at his January 1963 inauguration. These hostile words only made Dr. King more determined to seek racial equality.

King and the SCLC soon took their fight for justice to Birmingham, Alabama—a city, King said, "where brutality directed against Negroes was an unquestioned and unchallenged reality." The SCLC started this protest by asking blacks to boycott downtown stores until a list of demands was met. The demands included desegregating rest rooms and food counters, hiring more black employees, and opening parks and other city facilities to all races.

The SCLC also organized protest marches. In one march in April 1963, the police arrested King, saying he was violating a court order that prohibited public demonstrations in Birmingham. The Commissioner of Safety, Eugene "Bull" Connor, then ordered the police to put King and Abernathy in jail and keep them in solitary confinement.

While King was in jail, civil rights organizers planned "The Children's Crusade"—a peaceful march by Birmingham's children. They knew the marchers would be arrested. It was King's hope that the sight of children being arrested for marching

A Long Letter

During the eight days of his solitary confinement in the Birmingham jail, Dr. King used his time well. With only scraps of newspaper and toilet paper to write on, he composed a long letter to clergymen who thought his marches were too extreme. The resulting letter, which was dated April 16, 1963, was as long as this book and clearly stated the case for civil rights. "We have waited for more than 340 years for our constitutional and God-given rights," he wrote. "**Oppressed** people cannot remain oppressed forever."

After his release, King's "Letter from the Birmingham Jail" was published widely. It attracted thousands more supporters to the cause, and it stands today as one of the most important human rights documents of all time.

peacefully would win the support of more adults. "Our goal," he said, "is to fill the jails until these evil laws can no longer be used against us."

On May 2, 1963, teenagers gathered in small groups in downtown Birmingham. They merged with their siblings—many as young as seven and eight years old—and formed a demonstration large enough to disrupt traffic. That day, the Birmingham police arrested and jailed nearly one thousand youngsters.

The next day, however, more children showed up to march. Dr. King gave them a pep talk. "Don't get tired, don't get bitter," he encouraged them. What happened next, no one believed was possible. Bull Connor's police force attacked the children! Using vicious dogs and powerful, high-blast fire hoses, they knocked children to the ground. They used so much force that children's clothes were torn off and youngsters were flattened against buildings. Knocked down like bowling pins, the children were bleeding and terrified. Surveying the scene, Connor remarked with great satisfaction, "Look at those niggers run."

Americans who watched television that night saw images of Birmingham's police attacking children. They were stunned and outraged at Connor's disgraceful display of brute force. Connor's tactics had backfired

In 1963, the Birmingham, Alabama, police used high-pressure spray from fire hoses to break up demonstrations.

on him. Instead of ending the protests, his tactics hurt his segregationist cause and unified the nation in a fight against racial injustice.

The protests continued every day until the jails in Birmingham were full. By then, more than three thousand adults and children had been arrested. King was pleased. He saw the overflowing jails as "a magnificent expression of the determination of the Negro and a marvelous way to lay the whole issue before the conscience of the local and national community."

Policemen also used dogs in 1963 to intimidate and chase protesters in Birmingham.

Meanwhile, the boycott of downtown stores by blacks continued. Their nonviolent protest disrupted downtown traffic, scared off white customers, and nearly ruined Birmingham's economy. It was not long before the white businessmen wanted to negotiate. On May 10, 1963, store owners agreed to all of the SCLC's demands.

Love Your Brother

Dr. King drew on his understanding of the teachings of Gandhi, the Bible, and Thoreau when he spoke after the attack on Birmingham's children. "We must say to our white brothers all over the South who try to keep us down: We will match your capacity to inflict suffering with our capacity to endure suffering. We will meet your physical force with soul force. We will not hate you. And yet we cannot in all good conscience obey your evil laws. Do to us what you will. Threaten our children and we will still love you.... Bomb our homes ... and we will still love you. We will wear you down by our capacity to suffer."

They agreed to desegregate eating areas, bathrooms, water fountains, and dressing rooms in stores. They also agreed to hire African Americans in better-paying jobs and release those in jail.

After the agreement was signed, angry whites turned violent. President John F. Kennedy responded quickly, sending federal troops to Birmingham to restore order. Just a few weeks later, he addressed the nation: "We say we are the land of the free. We are, except for the Negroes. The time has come for America to remove the blight of racial discrimination and fulfill her promise [that all men are created equal]."

In August 1963, 200,000 civil rights marchers gathered in Washington, D.C., to demand equal treatment for African Americans.

CHAPTER 6

In June 1963, President Kennedy announced that he was submitting a new civil rights bill to Congress. "Race," Kennedy proclaimed, "has no place in American life or law."

A MARCH FOR FREEDOM

The time seemed right for people of all races to show support for civil rights. With that in mind, African-American leaders planned a one-day "March on Washington." It was intended as a peaceful rally to show unity, but no one knew how many people would show up or how the crowds would behave. As the day approached, almost everyone in Washington, D.C., was nervous.

President John F. Kennedy (fourth from right) met with civil rights leaders in August 1963.

On August 28, 1963, more than 250,000 peaceful civil rights supporters converged on the U.S. capital. Black and white, rich and poor, all people stood together for their common cause. Many sang songs and waved signs that said "We March For Jobs For All Now!" and "We Demand Voting Rights Now!" The marchers proceeded up the National Mall to the Lincoln Memorial. There, they heard speeches by distinguished civil rights leaders. Later, black singer Mahalia Jackson electrified the crowd with her heartfelt rendition of a well-known gospel song.

When Ms. Jackson's song ended, Dr. Martin Luther King Jr. began to speak. "I am happy to join with you today," he told the crowd, "in what will go down in history as the greatest demonstration for freedom in the history of our nation." Thus began King's now-famous "I Have a Dream" speech—a speech that rocked the enormous crowd. Fifty years later, it is still considered one of the most inspiring orations of the twentieth century.

"I Have a Dream"

Here is the most famous portion of Dr. King's speech.

"I have a dream that one day this nation will rise up and live out the true meaning of its creed: 'We hold these truths to be self-evident – that all men are created equal.' I have a dream that one day on the red hills of Georgia sons of former slaves and the sons of former slave owners will be able to sit down together at the table of brotherhood. . . . I have a dream that my four little children will one day live in a nation where they will not be judged by the color of their skin but by the content of their character. I have a dream today. . . . When we allow freedom to ring, when we let it ring from every village and every hamlet, from every state and every city, we will be able to speed up that day when all of God's children, black men and white men, Jews and Gentiles, Protestants and Catholics, will be able to join hands and sing in the words of the old Negro spiritual, "Free at last, Free at last! Thank God Almighty, we are free at last!"

Dr. King delivered his magnificent "I Have a Dream" speech on August 28, 1963.

The March on Washington successfully focused national attention on civil rights reform. The size and dignity of the crowd also impressed legislators in Congress—the people who were to vote on President Kennedy's Civil Rights bill.

Three weeks later, however, another bomb exploded in Birmingham. It killed four schoolgirls as they prepared for choir practice at Sixteenth Street Baptist Church. More death followed when President Kennedy was assassinated in Dallas, Texas, on November 22, 1963. Watching the tragic events unfold on television, King turned to his wife and said, "I don't think I'm going to live to reach forty. This is what is going to happen to me also."

Speaking in 1963, Malcolm X said that blacks and whites should be equal but should remain separate.

Friends and Enemies

In January 1964, *Time* magazine named Dr. King their "Man of the Year"—a huge honor. By this time, the young African-American minister had met with two presidents, had supporters in the U.S. Congress, and counted prominent African Americans in the arts among his friends.

In spite of his popularity, King was not well regarded by everyone. Southern legislators and white segregationists thought King was a troublemaker. They tried to discredit him by falsely suggesting that donations to the SCLC went directly into his pocket. Even the head of the Federal Bureau of Investigation (FBI), J. Edgar Hoover, tried to find evidence to dishonor King. Having a personal dislike of King, Hoover ordered wiretaps on his phones. He hoped to find damaging information that would ruin King's reputation.

King also had opponents in the black community. Malcolm X, the head of a black Muslim group, and Stokely Carmichael, the leader of the SNCC, believed that more violent actions were needed to seize freedom from whites. That criticism from within the black community hurt King most of all because he worked so hard for unity.

By the summer of 1964, President Lyndon B. Johnson, who had become president when Kennedy was assassinated, signed the Civil Rights Act. This act prohibited racial discrimination in public schools and in voter registration applications. It also outlawed segregated facilities in **public accommodations** under specific conditions.

President Lyndon Baines Johnson listened carefully to Dr. King when they met in 1965.

The Civil Rights Act did not bring about immediate improvement. In fact, the summer of 1964 was restless and painful in the South. The Ku Klux Klan continued its brutal assaults on civil rights volunteers in Florida and Mississippi, murdering three volunteers and injuring scores of others. Dozens of black churches were burned to the ground. Threats were made on Dr. King's life.

A SURPRISE ANNOUNCEMENT

Although the situation remained tense, an unexpected telephone call provided some relief in October 1964. The call came from Norway. The Nobel Committee was calling to announce that Dr. King had been selected to receive one of the highest honors in the world—the Nobel Peace Prize. King traveled to Norway in December to receive his award. There, the committee praised him as "the first person in the Western world

Accepting the Nobel Peace Prize

On accepting the award, King said, "I do not consider this merely an honor to me personally, but a tribute to the discipline, wise restraint and majestic courage of the millions of gallant Negroes and white persons of good will who have followed a nonviolent course in seeking to establish a reign of justice and rule of love across this nation of ours."

Besides prestige, the 1964 Nobel Peace Prize carried a $54,000 cash award. Instead of keeping the money, King donated it to civil rights organizations.

Martin Luther King Jr. posed with his Nobel Peace Prize medal in 1964.

to have shown us that a struggle can be waged without violence." The thirty-three-year-old King was the award's youngest recipient and only the second black American to be honored.

His critics were still unmoved. "They're scraping the bottom of the barrel," said Bull Connor, King's old enemy from Birmingham.

WE SHALL OVERCOME

Upon returning from Norway, Dr. King focused on voter registrations in Louisiana, Mississippi, and Alabama. The SCLC had already made some progress in registering black voters, but more than 80 percent of blacks in Alabama were still unregistered in early 1965.

Selma, Alabama, had a long tradition as a white segregationist stronghold. It also had the fewest registered black voters in the state. With those facts in mind, Dr. King chose Selma as the place to take a stand on voters' rights.

He arrived in January 1965 and began organizing. For the next few weeks, black men and women repeatedly tried to register at Selma's courthouse. The city's racist sheriff, Jim Clark, rebuffed them every time. Next, King organized a nonviolent march in Selma to protest voter discrimination. Because the group did not have a permit to march, however, King, Abernathy, and their followers were arrested and jailed. Writing from Selma's jail, King noted that "There are more Negroes in jail with me than there are on the voting rolls."

On Sunday, March 7, the situation took a violent turn. As King's volunteers peacefully returned from a march to their church headquarters, mounted police and state troopers attacked. "Get those goddamn niggers!" Clark shouted. Police used bullwhips, barbed-wire-

In 1965, mounted police attacked peaceful protestors in Selma, Alabama.

wrapped tubing, clubs, and tear gas against the frightened marchers. Many protesters fell wounded.

Within hours, "Bloody Sunday" began receiving nationwide news coverage. As in 1963, television viewers and newspaper readers reacted with horror when they saw images of policemen brutally assaulting Selma's women and children. This time, however, thousands protested in cities across North America.

King kept up the pressure. He planned a four-day walk from Selma to Montgomery, Alabama's capital. Hundreds of ministers of all faiths joined him on the march. When they

President Johnson Speaks Out

President Johnson introduced the Voting Rights bill on March 15, 1965, with these words, "It is wrong – deadly wrong – to deny any of your fellow Americans the right to vote. . . . We have already waited 100 years and more, and the time for waiting is gone." He continued, "What happened in Selma is part of a larger movement which reaches into every section and into every state of America. It is the effort of American Negroes to secure for themselves the full blessings of American life. Their cause must be our cause, too. Because it is not just Negroes, but really it is all of us who must overcome the rippling legacy of bigotry and injustice."

arrived in Montgomery, they planned to petition the governor for the right to vote and for an end to police brutality.

King received a permit to march, and the walk began on March 21, 1965. By then, two protesters had been murdered in Alabama, so President Johnson sent federal troops to protect the marchers. The group arrived safely in Montgomery and was met by more than 25,000 vocal supporters. Despite that backing, Alabama Governor George C. Wallace refused to meet with the marchers. He also refused to receive their petition.

Leaders of many faiths joined the march from Selma to Montgomery in March 1965.

The governor soon learned that he could not block voters' rights for long. The U.S. Congress, which had been watching the events in Selma and paying close attention to public opinion, decided to pass the president's voters' rights bill. On August 6, less than five months after King's Selma-to-Montgomery march, President Johnson signed the Voting Rights Act of 1965. That law, which has stood for almost forty years, protects the rights of citizens to vote by outlawing literacy tests and poll taxes.

A COURAGEOUS AMERICAN

Dr. King did not restrict his concern to racial matters. He was also troubled by the United States' involvement in the Vietnam War. American military involvement in Vietnam had begun in the early 1960s. At first, the United States had supplied limited support to help South Vietnam resist a communist invasion from North Vietnam. By 1965, however, the United States was engaged in a full-scale war. It lasted more than ten years, cost billions of dollars, and killed more than 50,000 American soldiers.

Dr. King was opposed to violence of any kind, so he believed that U.S. commitment to the war was morally wrong. Speaking publicly against the war for the first time in April 1967, King said, "I speak out against it not in anger but with anxiety and sorrow in my heart, and above all with a passionate desire to see our beloved country stand as the moral example of the world."

Monks in South Vietnam protested during the Vietnam War.

King believed that the U.S. government should not be funding the war but should instead be spending money to improve housing and create jobs. He also believed that money intended for health, education, and welfare programs should not be diverted to finance the war effort. To make that point in a very public way, he planned a Poor People's Campaign. It was to include a march in Washington, D.C., the next year—1968.

Between 1967 and 1968, Dr. King gave speeches around the country in order to raise support for the Poor People's Campaign. In March 1968, violence erupted when he went to Memphis, Tennessee, to speak. Several people were injured and one died. King was upset and angry. "Nonviolence as a concept is now on trial," he told the press as he vowed to return to Memphis to lead a "massive nonviolent demonstration."

Back in Memphis as promised, Dr. King gave one of the most moving speeches of his life on April 3, 1968. That speech, which is now called the "Mountaintop" speech, was the last one he ever made.

A VIOLENT ENDING

The day after he delivered that speech, Dr. King held meetings at the Lorraine Motel in

Memphis, Tennessee, 1968: Civil rights marchers pass between armed National Guardsmen and U.S. Army tanks (top right).

The Last Speech

"We've got some difficult days ahead. But it really doesn't matter with me now. Because I've been to the mountaintop. Like anybody I would like to live a long life. . . . But I'm not concerned about that now. . . . And I've seen the Promised Land. And I may not get there with you. But I want you to know tonight that we as a people will get to the Promised Land. So I'm happy tonight. I'm not worried about anything. I'm not fearing any man. . . . I have a dream this afternoon that the brotherhood of man will become a reality. With this faith I will carve a tunnel of hope from a mountain of despair."

Dr. King with other civil rights leaders at the Lorraine Motel on April 3, 1968. The next day, King was shot to death while standing on the same balcony.

Memphis. Just before leaving for dinner, he stepped onto the balcony of his room to chat with an associate who was standing in the parking lot below. Moments later, a shot rang out and a sniper's bullet tore through Dr. King's neck. The wound was fatal. King died at the hospital at 7:04 P.M. on April 4, 1968.

The black community was overcome with sorrow and anger at their loss. Concerned about the nation's response to the tragedy, President Johnson immediately went on television to ask "every citizen to reject the blind violence that has struck Dr. King who lived by nonviolence." In spite of this plea, rioting broke out in black neighborhoods in more than one hundred U.S. cities. More than thirty people died.

MOURNING

On Tuesday April 9, 1968, Reverend Ralph Abernathy delivered the eulogy for his

The Assassin

A week after Dr. King's death, police arrested James Earl Ray, a white racist and petty criminal. He was charged with King's murder and later convicted. Ray died in prison in 1998, while serving a life sentence for his crime.

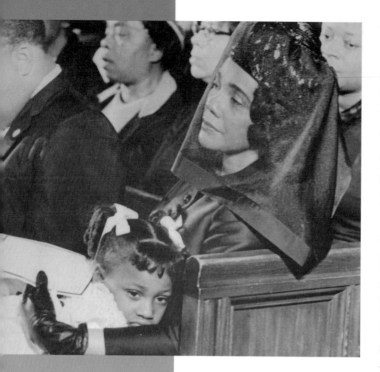

Coretta Scott King and her children at Dr. King's funeral in April 1968.

friend at Ebenezer Baptist Church in Atlanta. The mourners also heard a tape recording of Dr. King's voice that had been made a few weeks earlier. It was a recording of King's "Drum Major" sermon, a sermon in which King spoke about how he would like to be remembered. "I don't want a long funeral," he said. "I'd like somebody to say that day that Martin Luther King Jr. tried to love somebody. . . . I want you to be able to say that I did try to feed the hungry. . . . And I want you to say that I tried to love and serve humanity . . . say that I was a drum major for justice; say that I was a drum major for peace. . . ."

Tens of thousands waited outside the church in oppressive heat to pay their respects. Many wept as Dr. King's coffin was pulled through Atlanta's streets atop a simple mule-drawn farmer's cart.

Dr. King was buried in Atlanta. His tombstone reads simply, "Free at last, free at last, thank God Almighty I'm free at last."

CONTINUING THE CRUSADE

After King's death, Abernathy became president of the SCLC. He continued many of King's programs, including the Poor People's Campaign. Several of Dr. King's other SCLC coworkers were later elected and appointed to government offices, where they helped change unjust

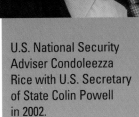

laws. Today, many African Americans hold elected and appointed offices. They serve as congressmen, governors, mayors, and state and local officials. And in 2000, Secretary of State Colin Powell became the first African American appointed to a cabinet-level position in the federal government.

Following her husband's death, Coretta Scott King established the Martin Luther King Jr. Center for Nonviolent Social Change (The King Center) to continue Dr. King's work. She also worked tirelessly to persuade President Reagan and the U.S. Congress to declare a federal holiday in her husband's memory. Since 1986, Martin Luther King Jr. Day has been celebrated as a national holiday on the third Monday in January. Dr. King was the first American who was not a U.S. president to receive that honor.

U.S. National Security Adviser Condoleezza Rice with U.S. Secretary of State Colin Powell in 2002.

Martin Luther King Jr. Day is celebrated each year on the third Monday in January.

Martin Luther King Jr. National Historic Site

The National Park Service maintains Dr. King's boyhood home, The King Center, Dr. King's grave site, Ebenezer Baptist church, and numerous other buildings as historic sites in Atlanta, Georgia, which receive more than 650,000 visitors each year

TIMELINE

1929	Martin Luther King Jr. is born in Atlanta, Georgia, on January 15.
1944	Graduates from Booker T. Washington High School.
1948	Graduates from Morehouse College and is ordained as a Baptist minister.
1951	Graduates from Crozer Theological Seminary.
1953	Marries Coretta Scott on June 18.
1954	Moves to Montgomery, Alabama.
1955	Directs the Montgomery Improvement's Association boycott against city buses.
1956	King's home is bombed in Montgomery.
1957	Elected President of the Southern Christian Leadership Conference (SCLC).
1959	Moves to Atlanta.
1960	Helps students form the Student Nonviolent Coordinating Committee (SNCC).
1963	Delivers "I Have a Dream" speech on the steps of the Lincoln Memorial in Washington, D.C., on August 28.
1964	Awarded the Nobel Peace Prize.
1965	Marches from Selma to Montgomery, Alabama, in a voter registration drive.
1965	Witnesses the signing of the Voting Rights Act.
1967	Speaks out against the Vietnam War.
1968	Assassinated on April 4 in Memphis, Tennessee.

GLOSSARY

baptized: a Christian ceremony that admits one in the faith.

boycotts: methods of protest against a company, organization, or government by refusing to use its products or services in order to force change.

civil rights: rights guaranteed by the U.S. Constitution that provide equal opportunity for people of all races and backgrounds to vote, and to work, live, and socialize where they choose.

discrimination: the practice of denying someone equal access to work, school, or a place to live, based on race, color, religion, or gender.

exile: one who is from his or her country or home, sometimes forced.

inferior: of less importance or value.

Jim Crow laws: rules that supported segregation and denied black citizens equal rights; named for the character of a black slave who appeared in staged entertainment shows in the 1800s.

Ku Klux Klan: a secret society that promotes white Christian supremacy by carrying out terrorist actions against minorities.

lynched: killed, usually by hanging, by a mob.

manacles: devices that restrain movement, usually restraints of the wrists or ankles.

oppressed: held down or back by unjust use of power.

philosophers: people who search for meaning, understanding, and wisdom in concepts, beliefs, and attitudes.

public accommodations: places used by the public, such as buses, trains, waiting areas, rest room facilities, food establishments, and parks.

segregation: the practice of dividing people into separate neighborhoods, work groups, schools, and public services solely on the basis of race, color, religion, or gender.

sharecroppers: people who farm land that is owned by someone else and who are paid a portion of the value of the crops by the owner.

sit-ins: protests in which people occupy seats of a racially segregated establishment in an attempt to force policy changes.

TO FIND OUT MORE

BOOKS

de Kay, James, *Meet Martin Luther King, Jr. Landmark Book* series. New York: Random House, 2001.

Downing, David. *Martin Luther King Jr.* Portsmouth, New Hampshire: Heinemann Library, 2002.

Farris, Christine King. *My Brother Martin: A Sister Remembers Growing Up with the Rev. Dr. Martin Luther King Jr.* New York: Simon & Schuster, 2003.

King, Martin Luther Jr. *I Have a Dream.* New York: Scholastic Trade, 1997.

Rappaport, Doreen. *Martin's Big Words: The Life of Dr. Martin Luther King, Jr.* New York: Jump at the Sun, 2001.

INTERNET SITES

The King Center
thekingcenter.com
The official site for Dr. Martin Luther King Jr.; it is both a memorial to and a continuation of his legacy as a great peacemaker and promoter of nonviolence.

Martin Luther King Jr. National Historic Site
www.nps.gov/malu
Run by the National Park Service, this official government site provides maps and information on how to visit Dr. King's boyhood home, the Sweet Auburn neighborhood, Ebenezer Baptist Church, and the King Center.

National Civil Rights Museum
www.civilrightsmuseum.org
Located in the Lorraine Motel in Memphis where Dr. King was killed, this building was transformed into a museum in 1991 to tell the story of the civil rights movement

Schomburg Center for Research in Black Culture
www.nypl.org/research/sc/sc.html
Part of the New York Public Library system, the Schomburg Center features one of the largest collections of African American literature and illustrations in the country, much of which is accessible in online exhibitions and articles.

INDEX

About the Author

Adele Q. Brown is an author with a lifelong interest in pop culture, art, and travel. She has written chapters for books on weather disasters, gardening folklore, and literary aliases. Her recent book, *What A Way To Go, Fabulous Funerals of the Famous and Infamous*, combines biography, pop culture, and history in relating the final stories of innovators such as Elvis Presley and Jim Henson. She has worked in the U.S. Senate, public television, corporate America, and with her husband in his photographic studio. Adele is based in New York City. This book is dedicated to her "rocking" nieces Kimberly Brown, Katrina Nelken, and Jordan Nelken.

3 1531 00254 1339